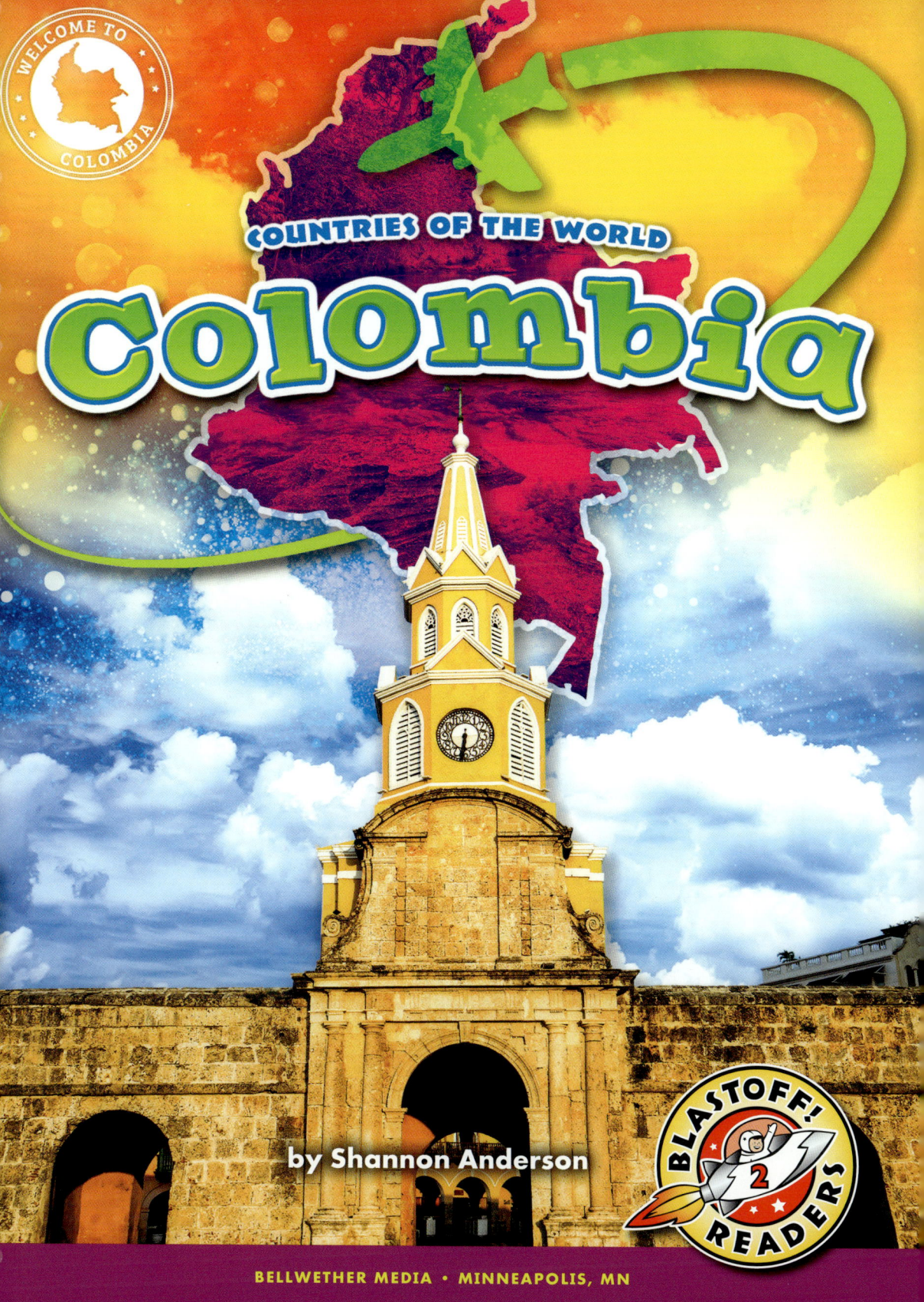

Blastoff! Readers are carefully developed by literacy experts to build reading stamina and move students toward fluency by combining standards-based content with developmentally appropriate text.

LEVELS

Level 1 provides the most support through repetition of high-frequency words, light text, predictable sentence patterns, and strong visual support.

Level 2 offers early readers a bit more challenge through varied sentences, increased text load, and text-supportive special features.

Level 3 advances early-fluent readers toward fluency through increased text load, less reliance on photos, advancing concepts, longer sentences, and more complex special features.

★ **Blastoff! Universe**

Reading Level

Grade K

Grades 1–3

Grade 4

This edition first published in 2025 by Bellwether Media, Inc.

No part of this publication may be reproduced in whole or in part without written permission of the publisher. For information regarding permission, write to Bellwether Media, Inc., Attention: Permissions Department, 6012 Blue Circle Drive, Minnetonka, MN 55343.

Library of Congress Cataloging-in-Publication Data

Names: Anderson, Shannon, 1972- author.
Title: Colombia / by Shannon Anderson.
Description: Minneapolis, MN : Bellwether Media, Inc., 2025. | Series: Blastoff! Readers : Countries of the world | Includes bibliographical references and index. | Audience: Ages 5-8 | Audience: Grades 2-3 | Summary: "Relevant images match informative text in this introduction to Colombia. Intended for students in kindergarten through third grade"– Provided by publisher.
Identifiers: LCCN 2024012101 (print) | LCCN 2024012102 (ebook) | ISBN 9798886879858 (library binding) | ISBN 9781644879177 (ebook)
Subjects: LCSH: Colombia–Juvenile literature.
Classification: LCC F2258.5 .A54 2025 (print) | LCC F2258.5 (ebook) | DDC 986.1–dc23/eng/20240325
LC record available at https://lccn.loc.gov/2024012101
LC ebook record available at https://lccn.loc.gov/2024012102

Text copyright © 2025 by Bellwether Media, Inc. BLASTOFF! READERS and associated logos are trademarks and/or registered trademarks of Bellwether Media, Inc. Bellwether Media is a division of Chrysalis Education Group.

Editor: Suzane Nguyen   Designer: Laura Sowers

Printed in the United States of America, North Mankato, MN.

Table of Contents

All About Colombia	4
Land and Animals	6
Life in Colombia	12
Colombia Facts	20
Glossary	22
To Learn More	23
Index	24

All About Colombia

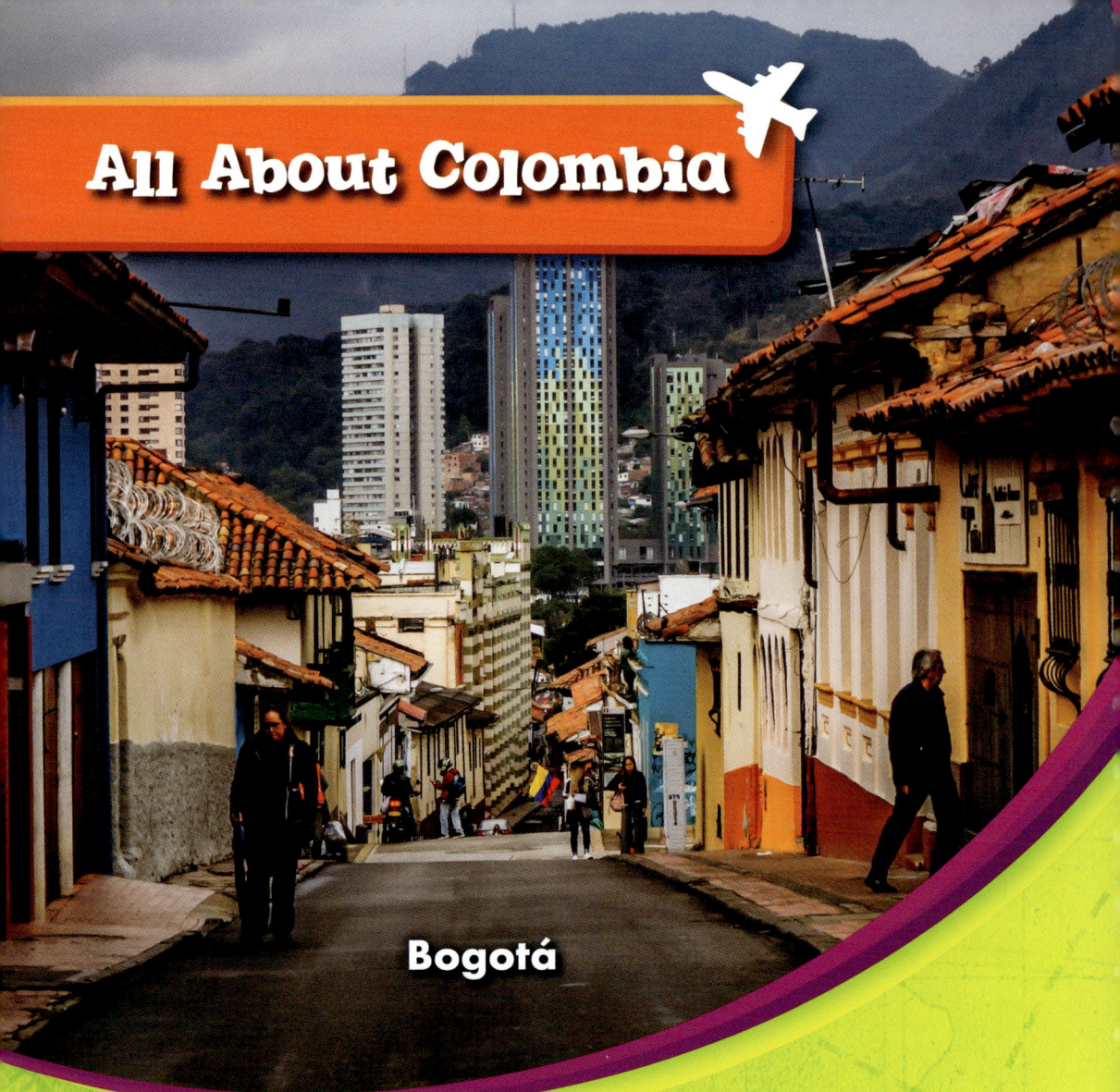

Bogotá

Colombia is one of the largest countries in South America.

Its capital is Bogotá. Bogotá sits on a **plateau** in the Andes Mountains.

Land and Animals

Colombia has many **landforms**. In the north are **deserts**. Mountains and **volcanoes** run through the center.

Grasslands cover the east. The south is full of thick forests.

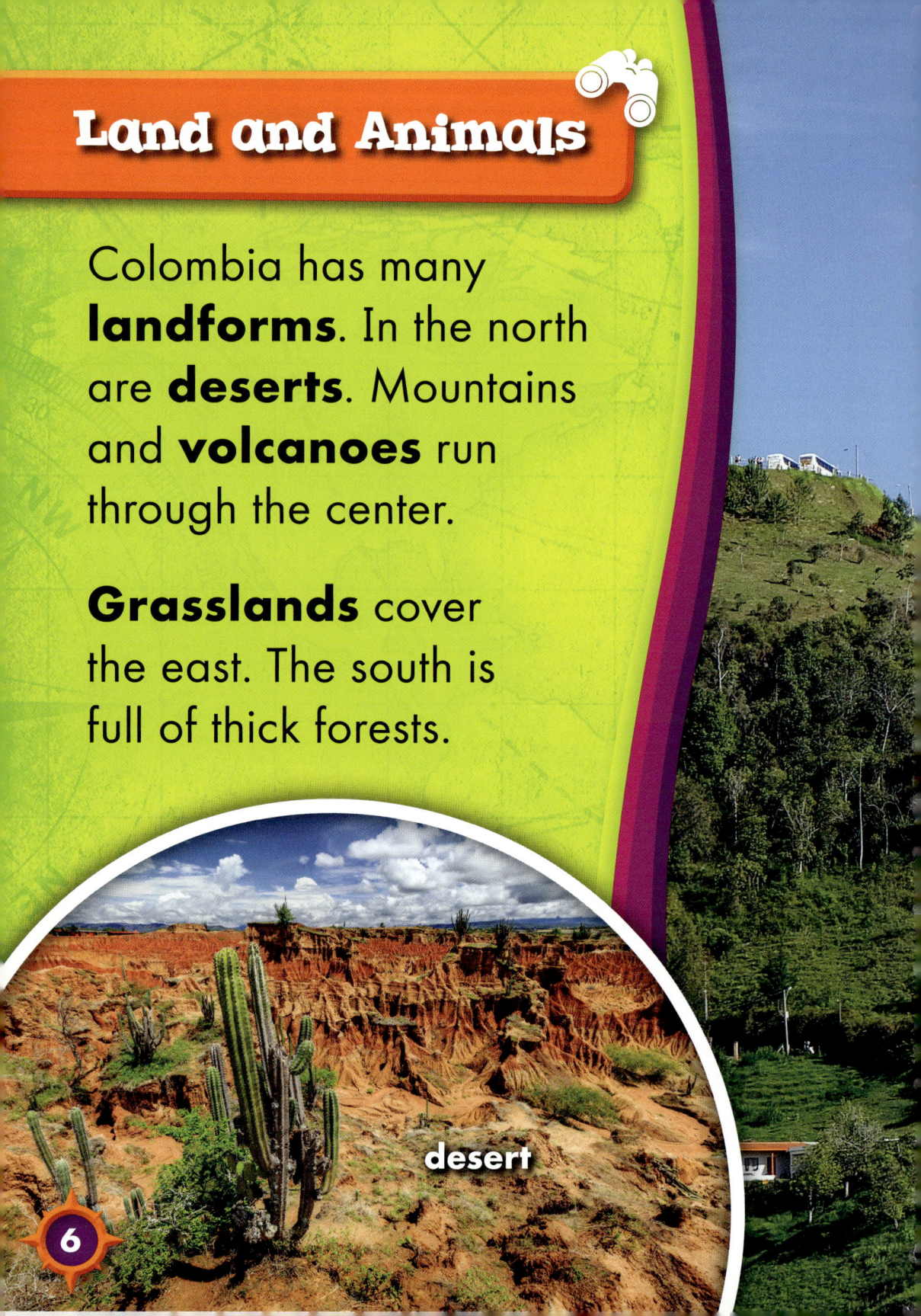

desert

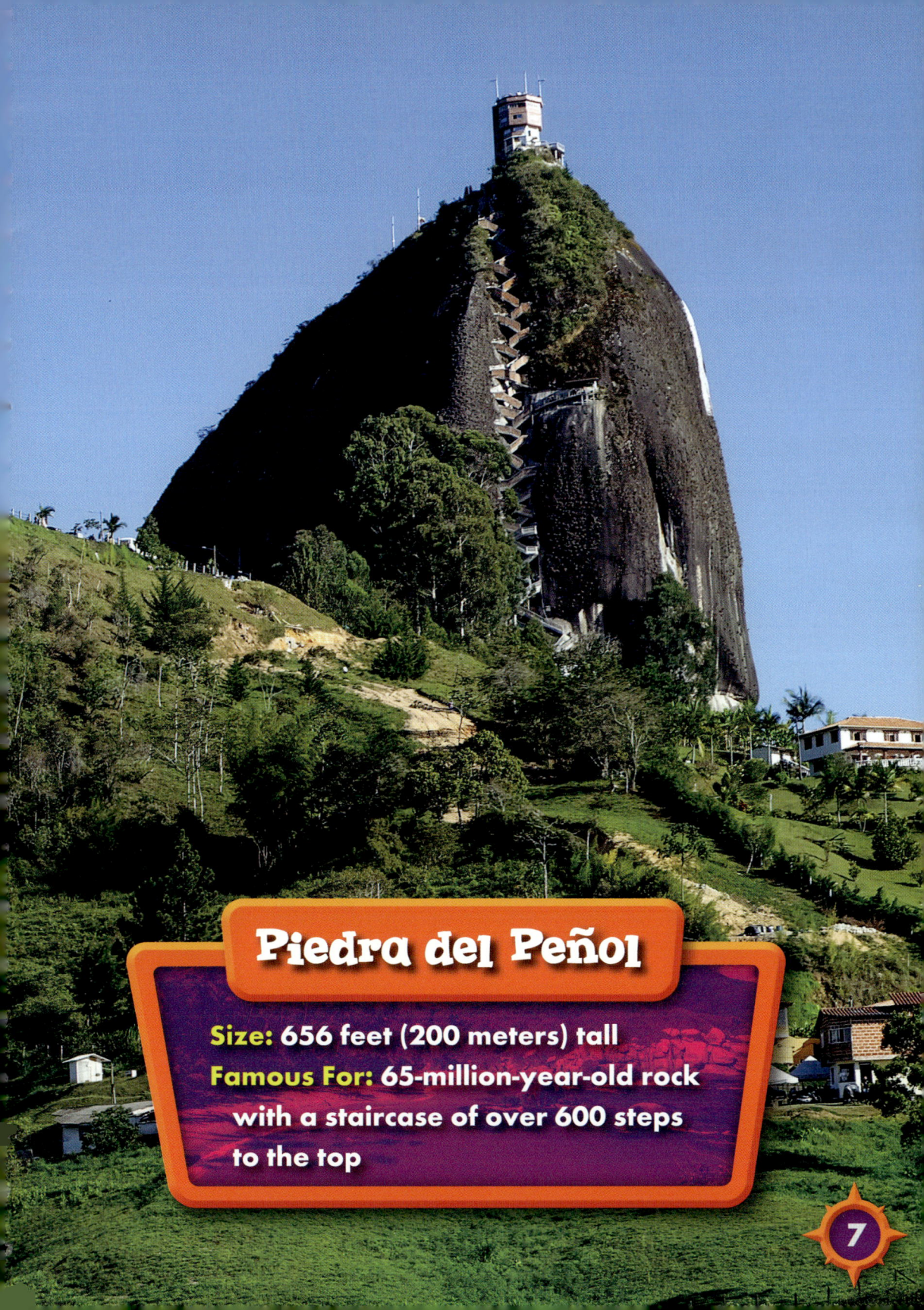

Piedra del Peñol

Size: 656 feet (200 meters) tall
Famous For: 65-million-year-old rock with a staircase of over 600 steps to the top

Colombia is located near the **equator**. It is warm there.

Most of the country has wet and dry seasons. The **tropical** forests receive a lot of rain.

Most animals live in forests.
Jaguars hunt for food.
Sloths rest in trees.

Brown-throated sloth

Animals of Colombia

jaguar

Brown-throated sloth

poison dart frog

Andean bear

Poison dart frogs warn enemies with their bright colors. Andean bears walk the mountains.

Life in Colombia

Most Colombians live in cities. They speak Spanish. Most people are **Catholics**.

Colombian families are often large. People value time with family.

Catholic church

soccer

Soccer is the most popular sport in Colombia. People also like to bike and race cars.

They enjoy many types of music. Some Colombians practice basket weaving.

basket weaving

Plantains are grown all over Colombia. They are like bananas. People fry them.

Colombian Foods

plantains

arroz con coco

ajiaco

coffee

Arroz con coco is coconut rice. *Ajiaco* is a popular stew. Colombians also enjoy drinking a lot of coffee.

Barranquilla Carnival

Colombians wear colorful costumes for the Barranquilla Carnival. Millions of people **celebrate** it each year.

18

They also celebrate New Year's Day. They spend time with family!

Colombia Facts

Size:
439,736 square miles
(1,138,911 square kilometers)

Population:
49,336,454 (2023)

National Holiday:
Independence Day (July 20)

Main Language:
Spanish

Capital City:
Bogotá

Famous Face

Name: Shakira

Famous For: award-winning singer born in Colombia

Religions

Catholic 92%
other 8%

Top Landmarks

Cocora Valley

Salt Cathedral of Zipaquirá

Tayrona National Park

Glossary

Catholics—people belonging or relating to the Christian church that is led by the pope

celebrate—to do something special or fun for an event, occasion, or holiday

deserts—dry lands with few plants and little rainfall

equator—the imaginary line around the center of the earth

grasslands—lands covered with grasses and other soft plants with few bushes or trees

landforms—natural features on Earth's surface; mountains and valleys are landforms.

plateau—a flat, raised area of land

tropical—having to do with a place that is hot and wet

volcanoes—holes in the earth; when a volcano erupts, hot ash, gas, or melted rock called lava shoots out.

To Learn More

AT THE LIBRARY

Isabel Sanchez Vegara, Maria. *Shakira*. London, U.K.: Frances Lincoln Children's Books, 2023.

Klepeis, Alicia Z. *Jaguars*. Minneapolis, Minn.: Bellwether Media, 2024.

Mather, Charis. *A Visit to Colombia*. Minneapolis, Minn.: Bearport Publishing Company, 2024.

ON THE WEB

FACTSURFER

Factsurfer.com gives you a safe, fun way to find more information.

1. Go to www.factsurfer.com.

2. Enter "Colombia" into the search box and click 🔍.

3. Select your book cover to see a list of related content.

Index

Andes Mountains, 5
animals, 10, 11
Barranquilla Carnival, 18
basket weaving, 15
bike, 14
Bogotá, 4, 5
capital (see Bogotá)
cars, 14
Catholics, 12
cities, 12
Colombia facts, 20–21
deserts, 6
equator, 8
family, 12, 19
food, 16, 17
forests, 6, 9, 10
grasslands, 6
landforms, 6
map, 5
mountains, 5, 6, 11

music, 15
New Year's Day, 19
people, 12, 14, 15, 16, 17, 18, 19
Piedra del Peñol, 7
plateau, 5
rain, 9
say hello, 13
seasons, 9
soccer, 14
South America, 4
Spanish, 12, 13
volcanoes, 6

The images in this book are reproduced through the courtesy of: Jess Kraft, front cover, p. 21 (Tayrona National Park); Mini Onion, p. 3; Gabriel Leonardo Guerrero, pp. 4-5; sunsinger, p. 6; John Rincon, pp. 6-7; OSTILL is Franck Camhi, pp. 8-9, 18-19; Jacques Jangoux/ Alamy, p. 9; Milan Zygmunt, pp. 10-11, 11 (sloth); reisegraf. ch, p. 11 (jaguar); Thorsten Spoerlein, p. 11 (Poison dart frog); Adilson Sochodolak, p. 11 (Andean bear); Saraponsphoto, pp. 12, 14-15; Bella Falk/ Alamy, pp. 12-13; hanohiki, p. 14; B Christopher/ Alamy, p. 15 (basket weaving); Ildi Papp, p. 16 (plantains); AS Foodstudio, p. 16 (*arroz con coco*); Sokor Space, p. 16 (*ajiaco*); Denis Tabler, p. 16 (coffee); seto contreras, p. 17; Faievych Vasyl, p. 20 (flag); ZUMA Press, Inc./ Alamy, p. 20 (Shakira); Danaan, p. 21 (Cocora Valley); Felix Lipov, p. 21 (Salt Cathedral of Zipaquirá); Christian Musat, p. 22.